Telushkinisms

Wisdom to the Point

Joseph Telushkin

SINAI LIVE BOOKS

Imprint of Rethink Partners, LLC

Rethink Partners books may be purchased for educational, business or sales promotional use. For more information please contact Rethink Partners, LLC at info@rethinkpartners.com.

ISBN-13: 978-0615610283
ISBN-10: 0615610285

Joseph Telushkin, is a rabbi, lecturer and author. Telushkin's book, Jewish Literacy: The Most Important Things to Know About the Jewish Religion, Its People and Its History, is one of the best-selling books on Judaism of the past two decades. Rabbi Telushkin was ordained at Yeshiva University in New York, and pursued graduate studies in Jewish history at Columbia University.

Introduction

Albert Einstein is reputed to have said, "Everything should be made as simple as possible, but not simpler." That is what I have set out to do in this book. Not to convey abstract, carefully reasoned arguments, but to supply concrete suggestions of activities that can be immediately incorporated into your life (such as declaring a periodic complaining fast; see page 24), or offering new ways to view aspects of your life that ordinarily seem negative (such as realizing that sometimes having things to worry about is a blessing, not a curse; see page 18).

Another brief teaching suggests a way we can practice "Love your neighbor as yourself," even when we have never met or probably never will meet our neighbors (strangely enough, it all has to do with how we react when we hear the sound of a siren; see page 27). I also offer insight into why Judaism does not always mandate that we forgive people who hurt us (see page 30).

It takes only a minute to explain why parents should reserve the highest praise of their children for when their children perform acts of kindness, but practicing this teaching can not only affect the rest of your children's lives, but also can affect the entire world (see page 35).

Many of the truths that matter most are brief but powerful. That's what this book aims to convey. You can read the book itself in an hour or two, but the lessons it contains – largely drawn from Jewish sources thousands of years old – can bless and enrich your life for as long as you live. In addition, practicing the activities described inside will also make you a happier person. What more could one want from a book? So, please, start reading now.

• • •

Self

Who is Rich?

I want to open with a teaching from an 1,800 year-old book, *Pirkei Avot* (Ethics of the Fathers). Unlike all the other books in the *Mishna*, which consist of legal rulings, *Pirkei Avot* contains the ethical aphorisms, the favorite quotes of the Rabbis. My favorite *Mishna* in the book comes at the beginning of chapter four where Rabbi Ben Zoma asks a series of questions. The first question is, "Who is wise?" The answer is, "One who learns from everybody." Our natural inclination is to think that the wise person is the one who teaches everybody. Wise is the person with the very high IQ. But the truth is that when someone is always going around teaching, that person is not acquiring new knowledge and is going to end up recycling old material. If you are willing to learn from other people and from every encounter, you will become a wise person. If a person has an extensive education but is not open to learning from the people they meet, their wisdom will decrease.

Then he asks another questions, "Who is a hero?" The answer is not one with great physical courage, though that is one possible way of explaining heroism. The truth of the matter is that some of us do not innately have great physical courage and even if we do, we are called upon to exercise it very rarely.

8

My daughter Naomi told me when she was four years old she thought I was the bravest man in the world. This belief was shattered when she was six and we went to an amusement park and I would not go on a roller coaster. The truth is that the Rabbis answer "Who is a hero?" in a way that makes heroism accessible to every one of us. They say that a hero is one who overcomes his bad inclinations." We all have different bad inclinations. We all have different weaknesses. A hero is one who confronts those weaknesses and works on him- and herself. This is something we are called upon to do every day of our lives. For example, if you have a bad temper and you wish you had better control over it, you need to work on it Why? Because a bad temper is not a victimless crime. People who do not control their temper cause a lot of pain to others.

The third question Ben Zoma asks is, "Who is rich?" The response is one that is hard for most of us to absorb: "One who is happy with what he has." The Rabbis don't say one who has a tremendous amount of money, but they also don't say, "One who is satisfied with what he has." Because you do not have to be satisfied with what you have. Judaism is not a religion that has a strongly ascetic inclination. In every society in which Jews have lived, we have never been confused with the Amish. There is an openness to materialism within Judaism – with trying to achieve material success. But that is not the goal. The goal is to be happy with what you have. The reason is because if you are not, you are never going to be happy.

Human beings want everything. Studies have shown that no matter what people are earning, they have the tendency to think that if their earnings increased by 25% then they would be happy. Or they have a tendency to think that if their child was doing better in this-or-that regard they would be happy. Or, "I would be happy if this or that happened." Our wants are very great. We are never really fully satisfied. We have to learn to be happy with what we have because if we are not, we are going to go around all the time with a feeling of tremendous discontent. And that is really very unfortunate and unnecessary.

I'll tell you a sad experience I've had as a rabbi. I'll meet with someone who has suffered an irrevocable loss. There has been a death or an illness for which there is not going to be a full recovery. The person will say to me, "Rabbi, if things could only go back to being the way they used to be, I'd be so happy!" But I knew that person when things were the way they used to be and he wasn't happy. The great tragedy is that there are people – and this is true of many of us – who can discover happiness only when they no longer have it. Life is structured in such a way that we are all going to go through difficult periods. We are all going to suffer losses, some of which are irrevocable. And, of course, those losses are going to make us sad. It is imperative, therefore, that we are able to feel happiness with what we have when it is not a time of loss, when it is the norm. Our normal frame of mind and mood should be, "I am happy unless something bad is happening." Many people are the opposite. They are only happy if something very good is happening. Their happiness is dependent on the extraordinary. But life is not lived in the extraordinary; it is lived in the ordinary. We have to learn to be happy during the ordinary times of life.

• • •

Hopelessness

One of the questions the Rabbis teach that we are asked after we die and come before the Heavenly Court is, "Did you hope for the world's redemption?" Normally this is understood at meaning that it is our responsibility to do what we can to make the world a better place. That is of course one, and probably, the primary meaning of this teaching. But it also has another meaning that becomes extremely important during a time like the present, when there is a sense of economic dislocation and the problems of the world seem so overwhelming.

During these times, it is easy to become quite hopeless. The Rabbis are telling us that part of being a worthy person is to hope for the world's redemption, and to hope for good things in your life as well. Once you give up, failure will always triumph. That is why it is such an advantage to be an optimist in life and not a pessimist. The only people who end up accomplishing anything are the optimists because the pessimists have given up in advance. Once you become aware of all the reasons why something is not going to succeed, you will not make the effort anymore because you don't think it will help. Optimism is the precursor for improvement of the world and the improvement of our lives. The Rabbis say we are going to be asked, "Did you hope for the world's redemption?" You cannot pass the test of being a good person and improving the world if you have given up on the possibility of the world's redemption. Improvement depends on having that hope.

• • •

Self Worth

What are you worth? No one is going to come up to you on the street and ask you that, and if they did you wouldn't answer. The truth of the matter is that most people are more willing to tell others about their sexual life than their financial assets. Think about it! How many people know precisely how much your financial net worth is, Nonetheless, though we don't discuss this in detail with others, many of us think a lot about our financial worth, and equate our worth with the value of our possessions.

If you are the sort of person who tracks your investments on a daily basis, you know more or less the value of your real estate holdings, the balances in your savings accounts, and chances are you could, off the top of your head, more or less say what the rest of your financial assets amount to. If you are not the sort of person who keeps tracks of such details, in an hour's investigation you could come up with a rough estimate of the value of your holdings. Far fewer are the people, who when they hear that question raised – "What are you worth?" – think, "That is a stupid and insulting question!"

My father worked in the 1930's for Rabbi Meir Berlin, the president of Mizrachi, the organization of Religious Zionists. Berlin learned English as an adult and many times when someone learns a second language, they have trouble incorporating the idioms. I remember someone once saying, "How am I ever going to learn to speak English properly when I find out that 'fat chance' and 'slim chance' mean the same thing?" Rabbi Berlin was puzzled by an idiom he heard Americans use and it eventually came to infuriate him. That was the expression, "So and so is worth…" followed by a sum of money. When he heard it said of a certain man for whom he had a low regard – this was during the Depression, when people were poor – "So and so is worth three hundred thousand dollars" – he responded, "Yes, that is what he is worth, not one penny more."

The real question of worth is, "What are we worth to the people around us? What is our value as a human being?" If we continue to associate worth only with money, we are setting ourselves up for misery. If you hear someone say, "I am worth ten million dollars," what happens to that person when his investments collapse and he is then worth two million dollars? If he loses everything, then what is he worth? Nothing? Our value is ultimately derived from the fact that we are created in God's image. We are holy people. All of us are holy. Our worth to others is going to derive from how we act.

There is no shortage of children who come from very wealthy homes who end up writing memoirs or speaking of their parents in the angriest manner. Similarly, there is no shortage of people who grew up with poor parents who have given them the most precious gift parents can give to their children and guess what, it is not money, it is love.   And that is worth everything.

• • •

Optimism vs. Pessimism

A Jewish joke: A group of elderly men in Tel Aviv, all retired, gather together at a café and talk about the world situation. Given what the world situation invariably is, their talk is downbeat. One day, one of the men in the group shocks them all by saying, "You know what? I'm an optimist!" They are all taken aback. They cannot believe it. Then one of them looks at him and notices something fishy, "Wait a second, if you're an optimist, why do you look so worried?" And the man answers, "You think it is easy to be an optimist?"

Judaism, in its insistence that the world is moving towards messianic redemption, is optimistic. But Jewish history, filled with pogroms, expulsions, and attacks, is pessimistic. Because of Jewish history we are pessimists. Because of Judaism we are optimists. Hence we end up as optimists with worried looks on our faces.

• • •

Why Many Worries Can Sometimes be a Blessing

One of my favorite figures in the American contemporary Jewish community is Rabbi Abraham Twerski. In addition to being a Hassidic Rebbe, he is also a psychiatrist. Rabbi Twerski tells the story that when one of his brothers was very ill, he went to a Rabbinic sage and asked for a blessing. The Rabbinic sage blessed his brother that there should be an improvement. Before Rabbi Twerski left, he said to him, "May you be blessed with many worries." Rabbi Twerski was taken aback; none of us like having worries. In fact, we shudder at our worries. The statement demanded an elaboration. He said, "Let me tell you what I mean. The worst thing in life is to only have one worry. When is it that you only have one worry? When something really awful is going on in your life. Your worry about your brother is so great that it drives out other worries."

We would all like to live life without any problems. A friend of mine, Dr. Shlomo Bardin, used to say when people would complain about their problems, "You don't want problems? There is one place you are not going to have a problem." When we live, we are going to have problems. But as the Rabbi then said to Rabbi Twerski, but when you are blessed with many worries, it means that not one of them is terrible. It means that you are leading a normal life during the course of which there will always be little problems here and there. Rabbi Twerski left the encounter and said, "I always disliked having problems but now I have an appreciation of them." It is not so terrible to have little problems because ultimately it means we are living an engaged life. I bless all of you: May you have many, but not too many, worries.

• • •

Relationships

Gratitude: The Prerequisite Trait for Being a Happy Person

I was once speaking to my friend, Dennis Prager, about the subject of gratitude. I was making the rather commonsensical observation that being a grateful person is morally appropriate and being an ingrate is very selfish. Dennis made an observation then that has affected me ever since: gratitude is not only an important indicator of character, it is also the prerequisite trait for being a happy person. When you think about it, it becomes obvious why.

What is the mindset of a grateful person? "Look what so and so did for me, he really cares about me. Look how she helped me, she really likes me." At the very moment that a person is cultivating a sense of gratitude, he or she is also cultivating a feeling of being loved. Conversely, what is the mindset of an ungrateful person? "The only reason he helped me is so that now I am obligated to help him. The only reason she spoke to so and so on my behalf is so that now I have to do something for her." What an ungrateful person reveals is not only an emotionally stingy disposition, but how profoundly unloved they feel.

This is an instance where doing the right thing turns out to be the right thing to do. Because as you cultivate gratitude, you do not only become a finer human being, you also become a happier person. It is something we can do several times, every day of our life. There are people who are masters at remembering every not nice thing someone did to them. You know how much happier you will be when you go around remembering the nice things people did! How much more loved you will feel! And we all want to feel loved, and we all want to be happy. Start practicing gratitude and you will feel a big increase in both.

• • •

Declare a Complaining Fast

Some days I will come back from work: I had a productive day, things went well, I'm in a good mood. My wife is not in a good mood, it turns out she had a difficult day and she starts telling me about the problems she had. As I'm listening, I'm sympathetic. But the more she goes on about what a hard day she had, the more I start to rethink my day. And then I say, "You think you had a hard day? Do you know what happened to me?" And in ten minutes we are each convinced we are living miserably unhappy lives. And so we declare a complaining fast. For 24 or 48 hours no one can complain about anything. It is remarkable how just stopping complaining can change the mood so much.

For a lot of us complaining has become a way of life. There are a lot of families in which the relationships and conversations often degenerate into everybody trying to show how difficult their life is. What ends up happening is that these conversations put everyone into a bad mood because they really do feel that this is relentlessly hard. I know a man who decided to practice this idea of a complaining fast vis-à-vis his daughter. It all came about this way. He was lying in bed at night, about to fall asleep, when he thought about his interactions with his ten-year-old daughter since he had come home from work. He had gone into her room, it was a big mess, and he yelled at her about that. At dinner she showed bad table manners so he snapped at her. A bit later, he asked her if she had done her homework; she hadn't, and he was upset about that. Later, she did her homework, and showed it to him. There were some careless mistakes, and he got upset about that too.

As he lay in bed, he thought, if my boss at work treated me like I'm treating my daughter, I'd become convinced that he thought I'm totally incompetent. So he decided that for the next two days he was not going to complain about anything, about, or to, his daughter. And what happened very quickly was that he was able to get in touch with all the things he loved and appreciated about her instead of constantly focusing on all the areas in which he thought she needed to improve.

Once we get into that complaining mode, whether in talking about our lives or in talking about other people, we tend to see everything refracted through that. We are just waiting for the other person to slip up so as to confirm the truth of all of our complaints. But now, all of a sudden, for two days, he remembered all the things he loved about his daughter, her affectionate nature, her artistic talents, her intelligence, and more. She in turn blossomed because when she wasn't afraid that she was being judged over everything she did, she could start reacting more spontaneously.

One of the quickest ways to start appreciating happiness and all the good things in your life now, is to declare a complaining fast. Declare that for a set time period no one in your house – or just you yourself – will complain about anything. You will suddenly become aware of how many wonderful things there are in your life. It will also become a lot easier to love with joy the people around you. Including yourself.

• • •

Siren Law

Some years ago, when I was living in Boulder, Colorado, I was speaking one evening with Rabbi Zalman Schachter-Shalomi. I mentioned to him something that bothered me and that I was a little embarrassed about. Sometimes, in our apartment in New York, on the Upper West Side, I'd be having an intense conversation with someone and suddenly our concentration would be shattered by the sound of an ambulance siren. My first reaction was to feel annoyed. Even though I knew that this was an inappropriate reaction, that is what would often happen.

Reb Zalman gave me advice, which I've tried to practice ever since: Whenever your attention is broken by a siren, stop whatever you are doing and pray for the person being affected. If it is someone in an ambulance, offer a prayer that they get to the hospital on time and be treated properly. If it is a fire truck, that the fireman can get there and stop people from being hurt. If it is a police car, that they can get to where they need to go on time, and stop something bad from happening.

I started making those prayers immediately after this conversation and one of the things that happened was that I stopped feeling annoyed when a siren interrupted a conversation, because I had a concrete activity to do. But within days, I realized something else. I was coming to practice "love your neighbor as yourself" even towards a neighbor I never met or would meet.

Once I made this suggestion at a speech. A few weeks later I ran into a man who had been at my talk who told me: "A few days after your lecture I was on the highway and suddenly traffic came to a halt. I could see way up ahead that there was an ambulance and there had been an accident. Normally, in those situations, the thought that goes through my head is 'My bad luck,' which is pretty ironic since someone else has been in an accident, and I'm sitting there thinking, 'My bad luck.' I thought back to the suggestion you made because I usually just get more and more annoyed as I'm waiting for the traffic to finally go forward. For those next twenty minutes, I tried to pray as much as I could for the person who had been hurt in the accident. I do not know if my prayers helped him, but I know that they helped me because I became more concerned with someone other than myself. "

Next time you hear an ambulance going by, its siren blaring, stop what you are doing and offer a prayer for the person inside. It can be a short prayer, perhaps modeled on the shortest prayer in the Bible, the prayer Moses offered when his sister, Miriam, fell ill. It is five words: "Oh God, please heal her." Say it. We'll become finer people and we'll learn how to practice "love your neighbor as yourself" even towards those that we have not yet met.

• • •

Forgiveness

A question that has been raised a lot recently is, "What is the right religious response to a Bernard Madoff?" Is someone who might have lost all of their money or a significant part of it because of Madoff's thievery required to forgive him? What is the right religious response for that person? My understanding, based on the Jewish tradition, is no. There are two reasons. One is obvious and the other is not as immediately obvious.

The more obvious reason is that to our knowledge Madoff has thus far not approached the people whom he hurt and asked for forgiveness. In Jewish teachings, if someone sincerely asks for forgiveness for the wrong they have done to you, you are supposed to forgive them. You have to struggle with yourself. Sometimes it is not easy. Even if the hurt is not irrevocable, it does not mean that the hurt is not deep. Therefore, our Rabbis have said, the person has to ask you and if you cannot forgive them the first time, struggle with yourself, and forgive them the second time. A person is required to ask you up to three times. It cannot be all at once. They cannot say, "Can you forgive me?" repeatedly. In the words of Maimonides (the great 12th century Jewish thinker), if you do not forgive the person after three times, you are acting as a cruel person.

Madoff has not yet asked for forgiveness, so of course that is one reason not to forgive him.

However, even if Madoff did ask for forgiveness, and even if it seemed to be a sincere request, Jewish law would deem it optional whether or not to accept his forgiveness for yet a different reason. It is optional because the damage he did to many people is irrevocable. The money that has been taken away is not going to be replaced, and for many of his victims, the loss has been devastating. In addition, a number of important foundations and charitable institutions lost a lot of money. Some of these groups helped people who were in desperate straits to secure some of their most basic needs, including medical care. That money is not going to be there anymore. There is no obligation in Judaism to grant forgiveness when someone has done a great evil and cannot undo it.

The obligation that does exist is for people to think before they act. Josh Billings, a 19th century American writer, once put it, "It is easier to repent of sins we have committed than to repent of those we intend to commit." Before we do wrong to another, we have to think of the implications of what we are doing. If there is no exit strategy from that wrong, as there is not in the case of a Ponzi scheme, if there is no way to ever really make it right, or if the ways to make it right are so farfetched as to make it virtually impossible, then we have to think it through before we do it. All wrong is wrong, but inflicting irrevocable, and sometimes life-destroying, hurt on another is an even greater type of wrong.

Clearly the evil that was done by Madoff was thought through in advance. Money was taken from people that can never be replaced. The damage cannot be undone. I do not advocate that Madoff's victims walk around their whole lives consumed by bitterness, because in addition to having lost their money this will be very unpleasant for the people who need to live amongst them. But if you are asking me if people have a moral obligation to forgive an act of this magnitude, the answer is no. First, forgiveness has not been requested and secondly, the damage to so many of his victims is irrevocable.

To paraphrase Josh Billings: "The most important sins to repent of are those you are intending to commit."

• • •

Loving Your Wife

Amongst traditional Jews, the wedding is not only celebrated on the day of the wedding but for a week afterwards in a series of parties called "*Sheva Berachot*" (seven blessings). This refers to the seven blessings recited under the wedding canopy; these same blessings are also recited at the end of the festive meal each night during the week after the couple has been married. At one of the *Sheva Brachot* parties that Dvorah, my wife, and I were having in the days after we married, a friend of ours, Professor Reuven Kimelman, stood up to give us a very special toast. It is over twenty years since this happened, so I do not remember his speech word for word. But what he said in essence was: If you look in the Talmud, the Rabbis apply the biblical verse "Love your neighbor as yourself" specifically to one's wife. Reuven asked, "Why do the Rabbis go out of their way to apply this teaching to one's wife?" He said, "Let me tell you what I think is the reason. I have been at social events where I've heard men say things about their wives that they wouldn't say about their business partners if they intended to stay in business with them. And yet if you ask the man, 'How can you speak that way about your wife?' he will say, 'Oh my wife knows that I love her.'"

"The proof of whether you have fulfilled 'Love your neighbor as yourself' to your spouse is not if you think you have fulfilled it, but that your spouse thinks that you have fulfilled it."

This is an infrequently commented-upon aspect of the commandment to love your neighbor. Most of us show love to other people by acting the way we want people to act when they love us. But to really love your neighbor, in this case your spouse, you have to figure out what is it that they really need. Do they need tremendous and oft-expressed statements of love? Do they need you to be careful how you spend money? Do they need you to arrive right on time, or as close to it as possible? Do they need great physical warmth? Obviously people in one way or another need all of those things, but we all have more dominant needs.

What is fascinating is that at the time the Talmud was written, women lived in a very disadvantaged position in society. It is therefore very impressive that the Rabbis focused on the need to love your wife as you love yourself. In the far more egalitarian age that we live in today, this commandment cuts in both directions. Does your wife feel that you love her as you love yourself? Does your husband feel that you love him as you love yourself?

• • •

Teaching Kindness

A number of years ago, I did an hour-long special show for PBS. It was on what I call "Moral Imagination," and I tried to share lessons that people could incorporate into their daily lives. At one point during our rehearsals I turned to the producer and said, "If everything else is forgotten except for this one lesson, it will be sufficient." And what I was referring to is this lesson: Parents should reserve their highest praise for their children for when their children do kind acts. Children generally get their highest praise for one of four things: for their academic achievements, for their athletic abilities, for their cultural achievements (e.g, musical playing abilities), and in the case of girls, for their looks.

A child who receives his or her highest compliment for one of these things is pleased. We know that people need all the compliments and support they can get. But underlying the good feelings about the compliment is also the feeling that parental love is somewhat dependent and influenced by the child's accomplishments. It is good to compliment a child about those things. But if we reserve the highest praise for when our children do kind acts, we would raise a generation of people who would most love themselves when they are doing kind things. That is why incorporating this idea into your family's life would be so transformative. In the absence of this, we end up in a society where a parent who says, "My child is a good kid," is almost made to sound as if the child's kind disposition is insignificant and unimportant. But kindness is the most important thing.

If I could change one thing in American and Jewish life, if I could find a foundation that wanted to support one project, I'd love it to be a project that would influence parents to raise a generation of people who were praised for doing kind acts. It would end up having a transformative effect. Within a matter of decades, it would exert a tremendous effect because people would most love themselves and feel best about themselves when they were doing kind deeds.

• • •

Spirituality

What Would God Want?

A spiritual person is ultimately one who will, in a given situation, ask himself or herself the question: "What does God want me to do?" It sort of bridges the gap between spirituality becoming overly abstract and a religion becoming too law-oriented. We do not always know the answer to what it is that God wants from us, but asking this question will, more often than not, bring us to a better, and hopefully the right, answer.

I tend to shy away in my own life from an overly abstract understanding of God. What really interests me in a given situation is figuring out what would be the right thing to do and what it is that God wants me to do. So bring this question, "What does God want me to do?" into your daily life. Some Jews might phrase the question differently: "What does the *Shulchan Aruch* want? What does Jewish Law say I should do?" This is an important question, but in some situations the answer cannot be found in a code of Jewish law. That's why I think we sometimes have to personalize the question, thinking in terms of God Himself. A spiritual person who gets up in the morning and prays to God, and who might pray to God several times throughout the day, therefore has to try to think, "Why am I praying to God? What is God? And what does God want of me?" To a surprisingly large extent, when we ask ourselves the question in a given situation, "What does God want me to do?" it will, more often than not, become obvious what the right thing to do is.

• • •

Religious and Spiritual Life

One of the great problems that has developed in Jewish life is that the word religious has come to be associated in people's minds exclusively with spiritual observance, so that if two Jews are speaking about a third and the question is raised, "Is so and so religious?" the answer "yes" or "no" will be based strictly on the person's level of ritual observance. He keeps Shabbat, he keeps Kosher, he is religious. He doesn't; he is not religious. From which one could form the very odd impression that in Judaism ethics are an extracurricular activity. I say this as a Jew who is passionately committed to ritual observance.

In addition to the fact that Jewish tradition considers many of its rituals to be ordained by God, I can offer three other reasons why ritual observance is so important. One is that without such observances we are not going to have a sense of the sacred and holy. Anybody who has experienced a meaningful Shabbat knows that the sense of sanctity derives from the holiday's rituals. I'll give you one example. According to Jewish law, the Sabbath is inaugurated with the lighting of two Shabbat candles. Many Jews practice the custom of lighting an additional candle for each child in the family. I grew up in a household where this was done.

I was once speaking to Rabbi Dr. Abraham Twerski, who is a very prominent and wonderful psychiatrist. Twerski told me he grew up in such a household in which an extra candle was lit for each child, and said, "It was very powerful to me to know that because I existed there was more light in my parents' house every Friday night." One of the powers of ritual is that it speaks the language of poetry. All parents tell their children that they love them and they tell it to them often. Years later, many of those children end up in a therapist's office saying that they never felt loved by their parents. But this ritual with the extra candle can convey the same idea week after week in a powerful – though indirect – manner.

A second reason rituals are so important is for Jewish continuity. Over three thousand years ago Jews were freed from Egyptian slavery, an act that has influenced more movements on behalf of human equality than any other act in recorded literature. If the Jews did not commemorate that Exodus from Egypt every year in a Seder, that narrative would continue to influence people but we, as a people, would no longer exist. Rituals help guarantee continuity. I'll give you another example. Ask most Americans when George Washington's birthday was. If they are over forty five or fifty they will all know it was February 22nd because we all grew up in a time when Washington's birthday was a day off from school and a celebratory day. Ask an American under twenty and most won't know it; because there no longer is a celebration of Washington's birthday. Everything has been condensed into President's Day, which is supposed to honor all presidents but in effect ends up honoring none.

Imagine if a group of rabbis got together and said, "You know how we can increase synagogue attendance on Yom Kippur? Let's standardize the day. Let's make it the first Sunday in October every year." What would happen? Within years, I believe, there would be an enormous fall-off in attendance. Part of the power of a ritual is that you have to adjust your life to the ritual. If the ritual can be dispensed with whenever it becomes inconvenient, people understand that it has no intrinsic significance. In Jewish life, holidays have existed for three thousand years. In those three thousand years, they have never arrived on time. When you hear Jews talking about the holidays, they will say, "The holidays were early this year; they were late this year." But whenever they fall, Jews observe them. You have to adjust to the ritual.

Third, rituals can teach ethics. When I was growing

up in Brooklyn in the 1950's, there was far less *Kashrut* supervision than there is today. Today you can go into a supermarket anywhere in the United States and find thousands of products that have rabbinical supervision. When I was growing up, if you kept Kosher, and I came from a very observant family, you were punctilious about making sure all meat products were under rabbinical supervision. When it came to dairy products, by and large, you would go into the supermarket and check the ingredients. My friend Dennis Prager, who grew up in Brooklyn, said, "When I was six-years-old, the first words I learned to read in English were 'pure-vegetable-shortening-only.' It is a good lesson to learn at the age of six that you can't have every candy bar in the candy store."

In short, it is clear that for reasons of sanctity, Jewish continuity, and ethics, ritual teachings are very important. But nonetheless, at the heart of Judaism is the ethical.

There is a story in the Talmud that is probably the most widely known tale in the Talmud. A non-Jew comes to Hillel and says, "Teach me the essence of Judaism while I am standing on one foot." Hillel answers, "What is hateful unto you, do not do to your neighbor. This is the whole Torah! The rest is commentary. Now go and study." What people do not realize, unless they are reading the story in the original, is that the story is more radical than people think.

First, what the non-Jew said to Hillel is not what is commonly thought and what I said above: "Teach me the essence of Judaism while I am standing on one foot." What he said was, "Convert me on condition that you can teach me Judaism's essence while I am standing on one foot." It is in response to this query from the would-be convert that Hillel says, "The essence of Judaism is that what is hateful unto you, do not do to your neighbor." In other words, Hillel puts ethics in the true center of Judaism and acceptance of Judaism's ethical principles as the major criteria for determining whether to convert someone to Judaism.

That is how we know that when we speak about the centrality of ethics, it is not some newfangled idea to try to make a nice impression on Western civilization. It is the heart of Judaism. Anyone who insists that something else is the central teaching of Judaism would actually be falsifying Judaism according to Hillel's understanding and according to Rabbi Akiva, the two most prominent sages of the Talmud. Akiva felt as did Hillel. As he taught, "Love your neighbor as yourself, this is the major principle of the Torah."

• • •

Obligatory vs. Voluntarily Action

Most Americans are concerned about dieting. And this makes sense. A large number of us are overweight. When I speak to an audience, I'll ask, "How many of you have gone on a diet in the past five years?" As a rule, the majority of people raise their hands. I'll then ask, "How many of you have never dieted?" A small minority raise their hands. I'll say, "You are the people who cause me to violate the Tenth Commandment against coveting. I don't covet your house. I don't covet your spouse. I covet your ability to eat all the Haagen-Dazs that you want without having to worry about it."

There is a fascinating idea that is conveyed when one compares two types of diet. Let me start by asking what the Hebrew word "mitzvah" means. People who know Hebrew will say "commandment." Others will say, "good deed," because that's the connotation of the word "mitzvah" in Yiddish. The difference between commandment and good deed is subtle but significant. Commandment implies something obligatory. Good deed implies something voluntary.

Most of us assume that an act done in the spirit

of volunteerism should be regarded as being on a higher ethical plane than an act done because one feels commanded. On the other hand, the prevailing sentiment in the Talmud is, "Greater is the one who is obligated to do something and who does it than one who is not obligated." What was the reasoning of the Rabbi who taught this? Maybe he felt that if you are doing an act because you want to do it anyway, it is not as great, not as religious, as doing it because God wants you to do it.

However, I think there is another reason. When you feel obligated, you carry out the required act with greater consistency. Let me now compare two types of diets. As I said, the average American worries about dieting. When I ask people, "How many of you who have dieted in the past ten years have gone three months or longer without breaking your diet once?" maybe one person out of twenty will raise their hands. And this is true even though diets offer very concrete rewards. If you are overweight and you lose weight, you will become healthier and physically more attractive. Nonetheless, when I ask, "How many of you broke your diet inside of three weeks?" a very large percentage of people raise their hands.

Compare this with the diet known as *Kashrut*. *Kashrut* does not yield any physical benefits that we know of. I have never seen someone whom I haven't seen in a long time, and said, "You look great! You must have lost 30 pounds! What are you doing different?" And the person responded, "I started keeping Kosher." The truth is the Kosher diet is filled with foods like Challah and Cholent, foods that put on weight. But unlike the regular diet that is undertaken as a voluntary act, the people who keep Kosher feel commanded to do so. Because they feel commanded, they can go for years, they can go for a lifetime without eating foods that are forbidden.

If I am at a Bar or Bat Mitzvah about to bite into a piece of chocolate cake and suddenly someone rushes over and says, "Joseph, do not eat the cake! You will look and feel better!" The whole time I will be thinking, "When is this nudnik going to go away so that I can eat this cake?" But if someone rushes over and says, "Joseph, do not eat the cake! While they were preparing it some pork fell into the mix!" I would throw it away in horror.

I have a theory. If the American government would mandate that they had to put pork into chocolate products, I could lose thirty pounds.

The fact that we feel commanded can sometimes actually make it easier for us to do the right thing and to do so consistently.

• • •

About the Author

Joseph Telushkin, named by *Talk* magazine as one of the 50 best speakers in the United States, is the author of *Jewish Literacy: The Most Important Things to Know About the Jewish Religion, Its People and Its History.* The most widely selling book on Judaism of the past two decades, *Jewish Literacy* has been hailed by leading figures in all the major movements of Judaism, and has been published in a third edition (June, 2008).

In 2006, Bell Tower/Crown published the first volume of his monumental work, *A Code of Jewish Ethics: You Shall be Holy*, a comprehensive presentation of Jewish teachings on the vital topic of personal character and integrity. Richard Joel, president of Yeshiva University, called the book, "a gift to humankind," and Rabbi David Wolpe hailed it "as a remarkable guide to goodness." In 2007, *A Code of Jewish Ethics* won the National Jewish Book Award as the Jewish book of the year. Volume 2 of the *Code*, subtitled, "Love Your Neighbor as Yourself" was published in 2009 to great acclaim.

In September, 2010, Telushkin published *Hillel: If Not Now, When?* A biography of the great talmudic sage that makes the argument as to why Hillel should emerge as the great rabbinic figure of the 21st century. The book discussed in detail Hillel's open and encouraging attitude to non-Jews interested in Judaism and in converting. Telushkin is currently writing a study of the life and impact of the Lubavitcher Rebbe.

Rabbi Telushkin's earlier book, *Words that Hurt, Words that Heal* became the motivating force behind Senators Joseph Lieberman and Connie Mack's 1996 Senate Resolution # 151 to establish a "National Speak No Evil Day" throughout the United States.

He has also written *Jewish Humor: What the Best Jewish Jokes Say About the Jews.* Larry Gelbart, author of Mash and Tootsie said that "I don't know if Jews are really the chosen people, but I think Joseph Telushkin's book makes a strong argument that we're the funniest." Telushkin is also co-author with Dennis Prager of one of the most influential Jewish books published in the last thirty-five years, *The Nine Questions People Ask About Judaism,* hailed by Herman Wouk as "the intelligent skeptic's guide to Judaism."

In 1997, his novel, *An Eye for an Eye,* became the basis for four episodes of David Kelley's Emmy Award-winning ABC TV series, *The Practice,* and he co-wrote (with Allen Estrin) three additional episodes of the program. Telushkin was the co-writer with David Brandes and the Associate Producer of the 1991 film, *The Quarrel*. The film, an American Playhouse production, and the winner of the Santa Barbara Film Festival, was released theatrically throughout the United States.

Rabbi Telushkin was ordained at Yeshiva University in New York, and pursued graduate studies in Jewish history at Columbia University. He resides in New York City with his wife, Dvorah Menashe Telushkin, and they have four children.

Telushkin lectures throughout the United States, serves as a Senior Associate of CLAL, and on the Board of Directors of the Jewish Book Council.

• • •

About Sinai Live Books

 Sinai Live is committed to assisting high-quality teachers share their wisdom.

Our goal is to offer a spiritual road map to enhance your personal journey and elevate everyday life.

Contact us at info@sinailive.com.

About Rethink Partners

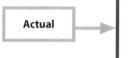

This reading experience was developed by Mark Pearlman's Rethink Partners, an organization dedicated to shifting user and industry perspectives through a combination of business strategy, product management, sales and marketing, editorial, design and online implementation.

Rethink Partners works with for-profit and non-profit organizations to help them reach their potential. We are focused on seeing both what is and what could be.

Visit us at www.rethinkpartners.com.

Rethink

Acknowledgements

This book would not have been possible without the help of many people. Special thanks goes to:

Mark Pearlman, for documenting Rabbi Telushkin and other world-class teachings on video over the past decade, for helping hundreds of thousands of people access these lectures at events and on the Internet through Sinai Live and JInsider, and for his initiative to create and publish this unique book.

Jake Laub, for his creativity in design and diligence in editing.

Raquel Amram, for her meticulous transcriptions and editing.

Daniel Schanler, for his expertise in video editing and production.

Made in the USA
Middletown, DE
07 July 2022

68728455R00033